Table of Contents

I0511320

"I am convinced that nothing we do is more important than hiring and developing people. At the end of the day you bet on people, not on strategies."
- Larry Bossidy, Author and Former COO of GE

Introduction

Why is it important for you to hire and interview effectively?

Whether your business is a large Fortune 500 Company or a small business, we intuitively know that your people are your greatest asset. Research has shown that you top performers are up to 400% more productive than average employees. You'll save time and money by hiring the right person and avoid the potential risk and cost of correcting performance issues later on, re-training, or re-recruiting replacements for them.

The average cost of replacing a talented employee can equate from 15% to 25% of their salary. (CBS, Inc.Com, & HR Magazine) Depending on the level of leadership, customer relationships and technical expertise they bring to your business, some say the cost can be up to 250% for a high performer.

This includes lost productivity time, lost knowledge, the work placed on other team members during their departure, recruiting and interviewing time, and the cost of on boarding and training a replacement. Every employee who leaves and must be replaced represents a significant cost to your business, therefore, it makes good business sense to hire the right person the first time, so that you don't waste time for money.

The Selection Process

Having a well-planned and structured selection process will help you avoid mistakes. We will review 5 steps in this book: 1) defining the job requirements, 2) reviewing application or resume, 3) conducting a pre-screening interview, 4) conducting an interview, and 5) selecting the final candidate for the position.

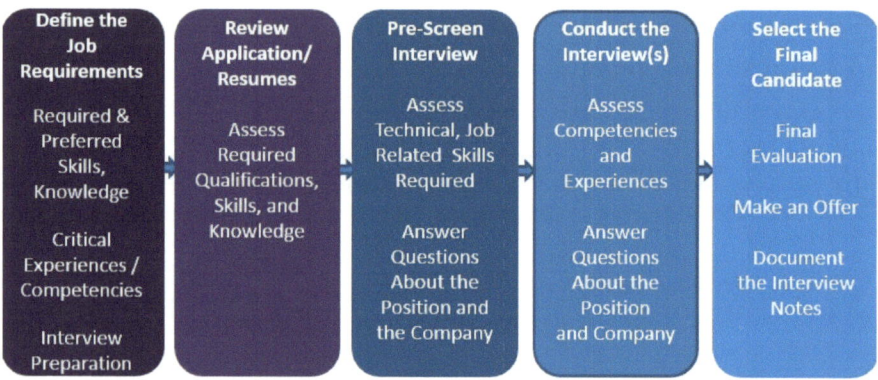

In the first step, you'll define the job requirements and distinguish required skills from those that are preferred, but not essential to performing the role. You'll also identify the experiences and competencies critical to success on the job. Finally, you'll prepare for the pre-screening interview process and interviews.

After this preparation and advertising the position, you'll review applications or resumes to assess the required qualifications, skills, knowledge and experience for the position.

Once the resume review is completed, typically the next step is a pre-screening interview conducted over the telephone, WebEx, FaceTime, or skype meeting. During the pre-screening interview, you'll assess technical and job related skills required for the role. This is also a time to answer questions about the position and company to ensure the candidate has realistic expectations.

If the candidate meets the requirements for the position, the next step is one or more interviews. Depending on the size of your business, you may have multiple interviews or a panel involved in the selection process. Prior to involving others, you will always want to ensure that interviews are trained on the requirements of the positions, as well effective and legal interview questions. During the interviews, you will assess the behavioral competencies and experience the candidate will bring to the position. It's also a best practice to allow the candidate time to ask questions about the position and company during the interview. This question and answer time will help ensure the position is a good fit for both the company and the prospective employee.

After the interview, you will select the final candidate, make an employment offer and document your interview notes.

Step 1: Define the Job Requirements & Prepare for the Interview

Prior to conducting any interviews, it's important to think about your current and future business needs and define the job requirements. While this sounds very simple, it's easy to jump ahead to selection of the final candidate without strategically thinking this through. We all know the power of networking when looking for work and are often eager to help friends and former colleagues find employment. A common mistake is jumping to the conclusion that a talented former colleague, friend or neighbor is your final candidate, before fully thinking through the responsibilities of the position.

Think about your current and future business needs. If your business is growing, you'll want to hire someone that has the skills to adapt to your future sales, market and customers. Identify and make a list of the required knowledge skills and experiences the final candidate must have. Then, make a list of the preferred knowledge, skills, and experiences that are nice to have, but not essential to doing the job.

You will want to define specific and measurable skills and knowledge necessary to meet the requirements of the job during this step. For example, knowledge and use of Microsoft Word, PowerPoint and Excel. Another example is knowledge and past use of process and tools for continuous improvement such as Six Sigma and lean manufacturing. Experiences include important exposure to certain types of work, projects, customers, or business situations, or the time in a job required to be effective in the role. An example could be including in your requirements an experience having designed and delivered a customer presentation or leading a process improvement team to a successful outcome. Use the table below to write down skills, knowledge and experience required for the job. Indicate if they are required or preferred by placing an X in the column.

Skill, Knowledge, Experience	Required (Must Have)	Preferred (Nice to Have – Not Required)

Define the complete responsibilities for the position. Identify the critical competencies and experiences a candidate needs to have to be successful in the role. Thinking about your past or current top performers and the competencies that have led to success will be help define them.

After defining the knowledge, skills, and experiences required for the role, you will also want to think about how you expect the job to be performed. For example, if you expect the final candidate to be able to perform the role with effective decision making and time management these would be important behavioral competencies to assess during the interview process. Additional examples of behavioral competencies include customer service, quality orientation, initiative, remaining flexible and adaptable to change, and relating well to other team members. Identifying behavioral competencies that will lead to effectiveness in the role will help provide a structure for selecting, evaluating, and developing employee behavior. Identify 3-5 behavioral competencies that are critical for success in the position. You'll assess whether the candidate has the required knowledge, skills, and experiences during the pre-screening interview and then assess the candidate's ability to demonstrate the behavioral competencies on the job during the in person interview. Use the table below to identify the behavioral competencies critical for success on the job.

Behavioral Competencies Required for Success	How do I want the candidate to behave on the job?

Create Effective Interview Questions

The best predictor of future behavior is past behavior, asking about hypothetical scenarios don't tell us how the person behaved in the situation. It's ok to ask yes or no questions on the application and during the pre-screening interview to assess whether or not the candidate meets the requirements for the role. However, during the in person interview, you really want to learn as much as possible about the candidate's behavior, so you want to allow the candidate talk about 80% of the time in the interview. Good questions related to the behavior you need on the job will get the candidate to talk about their experience and ability to demonstrate that behavior.

Prepare behavioral competency based questions to use during the interview, for example:

Tell me about a time when....

Describe a time when you had to...

How have you done this before...

Share an example of when you...

Sample Behavioral Competency Questions

Competency: Customer Service

Describe a situation where you had to establish a relationship with a customer within a short period of time. What did you do?

Share with me a time that you had to relay news to a customer that you anticipated would not be received well. How did you approach it?

Competency: Effective Decision Making

Tell me about a time you were asked to complete a task that you were unsure of what to do. How did you decide what to do?

Share an example of a decision that you made to solve a problem. What was the problem and what actions did you take?

You will also want to develop a good list of probing questions to refer to during the interview as you need more information. This will help keep you from leading the candidate by using phrases like "it appears as though you have... experience in ... is that correct?" Prepare a few probing questions to use when needed during the interview, for example:

Can you provide more detail about...?	What were the results...?
What exactly was your role...?	What did you learn from this...?

Legal Considerations

Finally, during step 1, prepare for the interview process early after you have carefully thought through the requirements for the position by developing a set of interview questions for both the pre-screening conversation and the interview. This work up-front will help you stay consistent and fair throughout the process with all candidates. If you plan to include others in the interview process, you will also want to educate them about the role and ensure they are trained on effective interviewing techniques.

Don't Ask: According to The Equal Employment Opportunity Commission, employers are prohibited from interview questions or making any hiring decisions which may have a discriminatory effect by screening out candidates based off of certain criteria. Don't ask questions related to race, color, religion, national origin, age, citizenship, ethnicity, marital status, gender, sexual preference, health or medical conditions including pregnancy. In fact, it's best not to ask for personal information at all to avoid unintentional bias during the process. Even rapport building questions should be planned carefully. Questions about irrelevant information like hobbies, church, or marital status, can lead the candidate to reveal unnecessary personal information that may bias your decision and lead them into revealing information that could be illegal to use in the decision making process.

Inappropriate Questions:

Are you pregnant?

Do you have diabetes?

How many days were you sick last year?

Do you go to Church?

Do ask questions related to the job responsibilities and goals for the position. Learn about the candidate's skills, experiences and behavioral competencies. Always prepare ahead of time and the same set of questions with each candidate.

Appropriate Questions:

This position requires working from 8-5 Monday through Friday. Are you able to work that shift?

This position requires wearing a uniform purchase in an assigned color to support customer satisfaction and professional appearance. Are you able to comply with this policy?

This position requires a high school diploma, did you graduate or earn a GED?

Are you able to perform the responsibilities of this position?

This position requires the ability to establish customer relationships quickly. Tell me about a situation in which you established a relationship with a customer in a short time period.

Step 2: Review the Application and/or Resume

You've done your preparation by identifying the responsibilities of the job and the knowledge, skills, and experiences that are needed to be successful in the position. Before you schedule interviews, you'll want to review the candidates' application and/or resume to find information supporting the skills, abilities, and competencies needed to have success on the job. This will help you narrow down the candidate pool and use your time wisely during the interview process.

When reviewing the information, focus on the activities and behaviors related to the job versus total experience indicated on the application or resume. Gaps in employment could be for many reasons, such as a layoff, personal reasons, or planned career change. However, if you notice frequent job changes, you'll want to assess why this is happening. Changes for advancement or development or sometimes downsizing are typically not a problem. Several changes within a short time frame such as less than a year could be a warning sign of potential performance problems.

Review all the applications/resumes at one time and rank all the candidates in order of preference considering the following factors:

1) Job related experience. Make sure they meet the requirements for the position, focus on activities/behavior they performed.

2) Credentials such as education, Diploma, Degree, relevant certifications, and/or awards received.

3) Gaps in employment. Don't immediately disregard a candidate for gaps, but discuss the reasons later during the interview process.

4) Frequent job changes. Assess why the changes are happening.

5) Writing skills. Look for a well written, organized, and easy to understand resume.

6) Salary requirements, if available, will allow you to assess whether or not the candidate's expectations are within your range.

Step 3: The Pre-Screening Interview

Most pre-screening interviews are conducted via phone. This should be a brief, approximately 30 minute, conversation. During the phone interview, your goal is to assess whether or not the candidate has the required knowledge, skills, and experiences related to the job.

Create a set of questions and a script to use with each candidate. Document job related notes during the interview and allow time to answer questions about the position and/or /company.

Sample Pre-Screening Interview Template

Candidate Name:	
Date of Phone Screening:	
Interviewer(s):	
Overall Candidate Rating on Expectations: Use a scale of 1−5 (1 = does not meet expectations; and 5 = exceeds expectations) to indicate the collective rankings of the interviews. A 3 rating is meeting the criteria for job performance.	Circle One: 1 2 3 4 5
Schedule Candidate for Face-to-Face Interview	Y or N When? _____

Initiate the Interview Discussion

Hello. My name is _____. I'm the _____
(insert title) for the _____ Department. Thank you for
applying for the _____ position.

During this interview, I hope to learn more about what you
are looking for in your next position and see if you are a good
fit for our team, as well. We will focus on your work
experience and expectations of the position.
I will be taking notes during the interview to capture our
discussion.

Do you have any questions about the interview before we get
started? Let's get started.

Gather Candidate Experience Details

_____ (use candidate's name), please tell me about your work experience. Only document work related information. Take time to clarify any additional work experience details.

_____ (use candidate's name), what interests you about this position? Only document work related information.

Clarify Job Requirements

Job Requirements *Only document work related information.*	Candidate Responses *Include any work related concerns.*
The scheduled hours for the position of _____ are _____(days of the week) from _____ to _____(hours). Can you work this specific shift?	Yes No Other:
This position requires, (list educational requirements):	Yes No Other:
This position requires:	Yes No Other:
This position requires:	Yes No Other:
This position requires:	Yes No Other:
This position requires:	Yes No Other:
This position requires:	Yes No Other:

Ask "Are there any questions that I can answer for you regarding this position?"

Close the Interview

Thank you, _____(insert name), for your time today. It was a pleasure getting to know you and learning more about your previous work experience. Tell the candidate about next steps in the interview process.

If you feel confident about moving the candidate forward to the face-to-face interview, schedule it at the end of the call. If you have concerns about moving the candidate forward for a face-to-face interview, tell the candidate you have additional candidates to review and will communicate your decision at a later date.

Thank you.

Step 4: Conduct the Interview and Assess Candidates for the Position

Prepare ahead of time and decide if there will be one or multiple interviewers and interviews. If you are having more than one in person participate in the interview, create a different set of questions for each person to use. This will give you more insight into the candidate's experience when you share information and the candidate won't feel as though they are repeating information during the process. Train the other interviewers ahead of time and make sure they understand their role in the process and the legal appropriateness of questions to ask during the interview. You'll also want to make sure they know to only document job related information in the interview notes.

During the interview, use the same set of 3-5 behavioral competency related questions for each candidate during the interview process. Stay with the process and structure. This will keep you from making mistakes or leading candidates. The most common mistakes are interviewers making decisions made too quickly, straying from job related questions and/or misinterpreting candidate information. Using the structured set of questions will also help you avoid unconscious biases and stereotypes. Feeling pressure to fill the role and hire someone quickly can affect your judgment.

Keep in mind at all times, it's much less costly to invest your tie in the process and hire the right person the first time in the long run. You will also want to avoid overselling the position to ensure you provide a realistic overview and select the best person for the role.

Establish a "neutral" tone toward each candidate. Nothing is more disappointing than to lead a candidate to believe they are the top person for the position and to then have them find out they didn't get the job. It is OK to let them know your process, for example you might say, "I'm conducting interviews this week with top candidates and expect to make an offer in the next two weeks or bring the top candidates back for a second round." Keep an open mind and consider opportunities for development in the candidate's responses. Look for patterns, themes, and reconcile any contradictions by using probing questions.

Remember to create a positive impression of the company for the candidate. You are representing your company to the candidate. The experience you create will leave an impression on the candidate. This information can be spread by word of mouth or social media to potential customers. You want to leave the impression that this would be a great place to work even if the position isn't the best fit for the candidate.

Think about your own interview experiences, what are some things that left a positive impression on you during the interview process? A welcome environment, offering the candidate a bottle of water, and allowing time to ask questions about the job or company are typical. A hurried, rushed process, lack of planning, interviewer running late from a meeting, or no follow up from the company to say a candidate has been selected can leave a negative impression and hurt your reputation as a potential employer.

The Typical Interview Agenda

The typical interview is about an hour long and begins with a brief introduction to the interviewer(S), job, and interview process. For example, you might begin with a 5 minute introduction, "My name is ... I'm the (role) for the ...department." If additional team members are present, invite them to go around the room and introduce themselves. "We appreciate you applying for the ... position. This position is responsible for... It's nice to visit with you in person and we sincerely appreciate your time and willingness to come in today for an interview."

Then proceed to prepare the candidate by describing the interview process, "During this interview, we will continue to learn more about what you are looking for in your next position and see if you are a good fit for our team, as well. We will focus on specific situations you have faced in your work experience. When responding, please pick a specific instance, details of what actions you took, and what happened as a result of your actions.   I will be taking notes during the interview to capture our discussion. Do you have any questions about the interview process before we get started?"

The bulk of your interview time, about 40 minutes, should be used to ask the competency related questions that you have developed for the role. The candidate should be doing 80% of the talking for you to learn about their experience during this time.

Then allow 15 minutes to close the interview and answer questions about the job and company for the candidate. Say "Thank you, for your time today. It was a pleasure getting to know you and learning more about your previous work experience." Tell the candidate about next steps in the interview process. Wrap up the conversation by asking, "Are there any questions I can answer for you regarding this position? Thank you."

5 Minutes	Welcome and introductions. Present information about the job. Share information about the interview process.
40 Minutes	Ask behavioral competency related questions. Allow 5 – 10 minutes per competency for the candidate to answer the question and to ask any probing questions for clarification
10 Minutes	Allow the candidate to ask questions
5 Minutes	Close the meeting. Discuss next steps in the process.

Sample Interview Template

Candidate Name:	
Date of Interview:	
Interviewer Name:	
Overall Candidate Rating of Behavioral Based Competencies: Use a scale of 1 – 5 (1 = does not meet expectations; and 5 = exceeds expectations) to indicate the overall ranking of the candidate. A 3 rating is meeting the criteria for job performance.	Circle One: 1 2 3 4 5
Recommendation:	Circle One: Hire or not hire

Instructions: Prior to the interview, select 2 interview questions per competency and plan to ask the same questions to each candidate.

Initiate the Interview Discussion

Hello. (*Shake hands*) My name is _____. I'm the
_____ (insert title) for the _____ Department.
If additional team members are present, invite them to go
around the room and introduce themselves.
We appreciate you applying for the _____ position.
The scheduled hours for the position of _____ are
_____(days of the week) from _____ to _____ (hours).
This position is responsible for _____.

It's nice to visit with you in person and we sincerely appreciate your time and willingness to come in today for an interview. During this interview, we will continue to learn more about what you are looking for in in your next position to if you are a good fit for our team. We will focus on specific situations you have faced in your work experience. When responding, please pick a specific instance, details of what actions you took, and what happened as a result of your actions.

I will be taking notes during the interview to capture our discussion.

Do you have any questions about the interview process before we get started?

Let's get started.

Questions for Each Behavioral Competency

During this section of the interview, I/we will ask you about more specific situations you have faced on the job. I want you to think about specific instances, rather than generalities, about when you had various work experiences identified in the question.

Competency 1:		
Question:		
What happened? When did it occur? What was your role?	What were the results or outcome?	What did you learn from the experience?
Notes:		
Question:		
What happened? When did it occur? What was your role?	What were the results or outcome?	What did you learn from the experience?
Notes:		

Competency 2:		
Question:		
What happened? When did it occur? What was your role?	**What were the results or outcomes?**	**What did you learn from the experience?**
Notes:		
Question:		
What happened? When did it occur? What was your role?	**What were the results or outcomes?**	**What did you learn from the experience?**
Notes:		

Competency 3:		
Question:		
What happened? When did it occur? What was your role?	What were the results or outcomes?	What did you learn from the experience?
Notes:		
Question:		
What happened? When did it occur? What was your role?	What were the results or outcomes?	What did you learn from the experience?
Notes:		

Competency 4:		
Question:		
What happened? When did it occur? What was your role?	What were the results or outcome?	**What did you learn from the experience?**
Notes:		
Question		
What happened? When did it occur? What was your role?	What were the results or outcomes?	**What did you learn from the experience?**
Notes:		

Competency 5:		
Question:		
What happened? When did it occur? What was your role?	What were the results or outcome?	What did you learn from the experience?
Notes:		
Question		
What happened? When did it occur? What was your role?	What were the results or outcomes?	What did you learn from the experience?
Notes:		

Close the Interview

Thank you, _____(*insert name*), for your time today. It was a pleasure getting to know you and learning more about your previous work experience.   Tell the candidate about next steps in the interview process.

Wrap up with the following question, "Are there any questions I can answer for you regarding this position?"

Thank you. *Shake hands.*

Competency Rating Grid (in rank order)		
Only document work related information.		
Competency 1:	Circle One: 1 2 3 4 5	Additional Comments:
Competency 2:	Circle One: 1 2 3 4 5	
Competency 3:	Circle One: 1 2 3 4 5	
Competency 4:	Circle One: 1 2 3 4 5	
Competency 5:	Circle One: 1 2 3 4 5	

Additional Probing Questions

The following questions can be used to gather more detail from a candidate.

Can you provide a specific situation?
What happened causing you to take action?
Can you provide a few more details about the situation?
What led you to...?
What were the circumstances surrounding...?
Who was the customer, team-member, etc.?
What caused you to react?
Specifically, what did you do?
How did you handle the situation?
What did you say?
How did you respond?
How did others respond?
Walk me through the steps you took.
What happened?
How did that affect...?
How did you measure your success?
What problems/successes resulted from...?
What was the customer's reaction?
What feedback have you received?
What did you do well in the situation?
What will you continue to do in the future?
What would you do differently next time?
How have you applied what you learned to other situations at work or school?

Step 5: Select the Final Candidate

After you have interviewed all the candidates for the positon, you'll want to spend some time to conduct your final evaluation and ranking of all the candidates. If you have involved more than one interviewer, invite the interview panel to participate or give input into in this process.

Consider the following elements in your final ranking and selection.

Education & credentials
Overall experience
Required skills and knowledge
Behavioral competency assessment
Potential to develop and learn in the role

Extend an offer to your final candidate and document the interview process.

Record only job relevant notes during the interviews. Whether you hire the applicant or not, it is critical that you accurately document the interview by writing only exactly what is said by the candidate. Write clearly and legibly in your notes and do not include any discriminating or biased comments, even notes like "blond hair", can raise questions. Note whether the applicant was hired for the positon and if not hired, provide a reason why applicant was declined.

Keep information for all candidates in a confidential file.

Conclusion

Having a structured interview process can save time and money in the long run when it comes to selecting the right person and retaining them. Review what you have learned, identify the critical knowledge, skills, experience, and competencies for each position. Think through the behavioral competencies that you need to have your employees' demonstration on the job and create a set of thoughtful interview questions. The best way to improve your ability to make great hiring decisions is to practice and observe great interviewers.

"When I meet successful people, I ask…what they attribute their success to. It is usually the same: persistence, hard work, and hiring good people."
- Kiana Tom